Injury Time

CLIVE JAMES

Injury Time

PICADOR

First published 2017 by Picador
an imprint of Pan Macmillan
20 New Wharf Road, London N1 9RR
Associated companies throughout the world
www.panmacmillan.com

ISBN 978-1-5098-5297-0

1 3 5 7 9 8 6 4 2

A CIP catalogue record for this book is available from the British Library.

Printed and bound by CPI Group (UK) Ltd, Croydon, CR0 4YY

To the nurses, doctors and staff of
Addenbrooke's Hospital, Cambridge, England:
with all my thanks for these unexpected recent years.

simplex munditiis

Plain in thy neatness.

– Horace

An author is not to write all he can,
but only all he ought.

– Dryden

Foreword

When I locked up the final text for my previous volume of short poems, *Sentenced to Life*, I thought, rather grandly, that there would be no time left except perhaps for a long poem that might gain in poignancy by being left unfinished. I should have known better than to flirt with the metallic music of downed tools. Before my avowedly last collection was even in proof, new short poems had begun to arrive, and after a year or so it was already evident that they might add up to a book, once I solved the problem of how to write about, say, the death of Ayrton Senna. (Surely an appropriate obsequy would need a thousand-horsepower sound-track.) In my experience, it's never a book before certain key themes have been touched on, but once they are, it always is, or anyway it's going to be. It helps, of course, to have a publisher who thinks the same; and on that point Don Paterson at Picador was once again the ideal mentor.

For this collection, I have kept the rule of providing notes at the end of the volume, but only if they help to explain factual points that might be obscure. If the note explained the poem itself, the poem would be incomplete. In my later stages I have got increasingly keen on that precept. Explaining itself is what a poem does. Helping me to be certain that any new project really did have something intelligible to say for itself, David Free, Stephen Edgar, Tom Stoppard, my wife Prue Shaw and my elder daughter Claerwen James saw nearly all these poems in their early stages, and often I would also run them past Ian McEwan and Martin Amis. Though not all of these busy people thought everything I had written was marvellous, if any of them showed doubts it was always enough to make me think twice. But the day has not yet quite arrived when circulation by e-mail will count as tending an audience. Print still rules, and finally the editors of the periodicals will have to see and judge what the author fancies to be a finished product.

Once again I must especially thank Alan Jenkins of the *TLS*, Dan Johnson of *Standpoint*, Paul Muldoon of the *New Yorker*, Tom Gatti of the *New Statesman*, Sam Leith of the *Spectator* and Les Murray of *Quadrant*, while welcoming a new and generous grandee to my range of principal editorial mentors: Sandy McClatchy of the *Yale Review*. I should also thank the *Kenyon Review*, one of whose operatives has only just now written to discuss a printing schedule for a couple of poems that I can't remember having sent. I go to sleep and dream of editorial ninjas breaking into my study and microfilming the MS of the unfinished epic in my bottom drawer. Remembering how wrong I turned out to be when I thought the poems in *Sentenced to Life* would be my last, I should say at this point that I had to think twice before giving this book a title suggesting that the game might soon be over. As it happens, I am writing this introductory note on the morning after an operation at Addenbrooke's in which items of machinery – some of them, in my imagination, as big as the USS *Nimitz* – had been sent sailing up my interior in search of organic damage. I would have liked to be awake, in order to pick up the running commentary of my lavish range of nurses and surgeons. Alas, the relaxing agent they had given me relaxed me all the way to sleep, so the only interesting dialogue I heard was from the actors in *Fantastic Voyage*, which, by a trick of senescent memory, had been running in my waking brain for days beforehand, and was now running, even more vividly, in the depths of my slumber. From dreams of Raquel Welch navigating between the platelets I awoke to be told that I could once again safely have breakfast.

Or perhaps even safely begin writing something new. And indeed even now, a full six years into the trajectory of my dying fall, I do still have plans for other books, including a funeral oratorio which might celebrate at some length the very fact that my confidently forecast imminent demise turned out to be not as imminent as all that. There could also be a clinching volume of memoirs, its credibility endorsed by the bark of a Luger from my study late at night.

But I can be fairly sure that I am by now more or less done with the short lyrics. They take more concentration, and therefore more energy, than any other form of writing. I used always to keep the rule that if a poem started forming in my head then I should stick with it until it was finished. Here in my hideout in the Cambridge fens, in the middle of a dreary winter, with the prospect of further medical intervention retreating only to loom again, that rule begins to look too expensive. I can still imagine myself, however, feeling compelled to break it. Finally a poem can demand to be read only because it demanded to be written, and it is notable that the dying Hamlet is still balancing his phrases even when young Fortinbras has arrived outside in the lobby. At one stage I thought of calling this little volume *The Rest Is Silence*, but that would have been to give myself airs. It is quite pretentious enough to evoke the image of an exhausted footballer still plugging away with legs like lead.

Cambridge, 2017

Contents

Injury Time

Return of the Kogarah Kid

Inscription for a small bronze plaque at Dawes Point

Here I began and here I reach the end.
From here my ashes go back to the sea
And take my memories of every friend
And love, and anything still dear to me,
Down to the darkness out of which the sun
Will rise again, this splendour never less:
Fated to be, when all is said, and done,
For others to recall and curse or bless
The way that time runs out but still comes in,
The new tide always ready to begin.

Do the gulls cry in triumph, or distress?
In neither, for they cry because they must,
Not knowing this is glory, unaware
Their time will come to leave it. It is just
That we, who learned to breathe the brilliant air
And first were told that we were made of dust
Here in this city, yet went out across
The globe to find fame, should return one day
To trade our gains against a certain loss –
And sink from sight where once we sailed away.

Anchorage International

In those days Russia was still closed. My flight
Would cross the Pole and land at Anchorage
To refuel. Many times, by day or night,
I watched them shine or blink, that pilgrimage
Of planes descending from the stratosphere
Down some steep trail. As if I'd come to stay,
I lived in that lounge, neither there nor here:
The still point of transition. I would pay
For drinks with cash, it was so long ago –
But now, again, it is a place I know.

I've changed a lot, but these seats look the same,
Except there are so few of us who wait.
It's like a party but nobody came.
There is no voice that calls us to the gate,
For no procession interrupts the sky.
It seems that this time I will not move on.
I have arrived. With nowhere left to fly,
I need not leave: I have already gone.
There's almost nothing left to think about
Except the swirl of snow as I look out.

Here in this neutral zone at last we learn
That all our travelling must come to rest
In stillness: no way forward, no return.
We once thought to keep moving might be best
Until we reached the end, but it was there
From the beginning. Darkness gave the dawn
Its inward depth. The lights in the night air
That came down slowly were us, being born
Alive. The silver points in the pale blue
Of daylight were us dying. Both were true.

I bought your small white boxes marked Chanel
At Anchorage. I must have used a card.
Did I? I can't remember very well.
In these last, feeble days I find it hard
To fix a detail of the way things were
And set it in its time. Soon there will be
Only one final thing left to occur,
One little thing. You need not fear for me:
It can't hurt. Of that much I can be sure.
I know this place. I have been here before.

Hiatus

In February, winter was undone.
Day after day a honeysuckle sun
Glowed in the windows. Though the nights were long,
And from one bird song to the next bird song
Took half the morning, still it worked like spring.
I breathed the yielding air and felt it bring
My lost life back to me, at least in part:
Enough, at any rate, to keep my heart –
The one intact component that I've got –
From breaking at the thought that I might not
Summon the strength to see the season through
And all the sweet world properly made new.

We old and ill must measure time that way.
When young, we scarcely saw the interplay
Of life and the surrounding atmosphere:
We just lived in it. Now the truth is here:
Existence wants us gone. The oxygen
We once wolfed down now fuels a fire, and when
The air is cold the flames reach deep within,
Reminding us that we can never win
This battle. Only let the air turn mild,
However, and the power of hope runs wild:
It makes a fool of me, as if I could
Begin again, and be both strong and good.

Another month, and still the freeze is slow
To come back to the lawns and wreck their show
Of ground-based blooms. But I have seen before
How March can throw a quick switch, and restore
The temperature to what it ought to be
In any keyhole not blocked with a key,
And how the caught-out flowers pay the cost
Of misplaced confidence. Felled by the frost,
Here without leave and gone without a fight,
Where do they go? They vanish overnight.
This time, perhaps not. Maybe death will take
A whole new attitude, just for my sake.

Visitation of the Dove

Night is at hand already: it is well
That we yield to the night. So Homer sings,
As if there were no Heaven and no Hell,
But only peace.
The grey dove comes down in a storm of wings
Into my garden where seeds never cease

To be supplied as if life fits a plan
Where needs are catered to. One need is not:
I do not wish to leave yet. If I can
I will stay on
And see another autumn, having got
This far with all my strength not yet quite gone.

When Phèdre, dying, says that she can see
Already not much more than through a cloud,
She adds that death has taken clarity
Out of her eyes
To give it to the world. Behold my shroud!
This brilliance in the garden. The dove flies.

The Gardener in White

The Reaper sobers you. You will be stirred
By just how serious you tend to get
When he draws near and has his quiet word.
His murmur is the closest you've heard yet
To someone heavy calling in a debt.
No gun, no flick-knife: none of that gangster thing.
Just you, him, and the fear that you might die,
As the fluff-ball tern chick under its mother's wing
Senses the black-back gull in the clear sky,
And shivers from the knowledge in its blood.
The end of life is like a flower's bud
Formed from the code of its unfolding bloom,
Which carries, in its turn, the burst of light
That lies ahead, the blinding crack of doom
When petals in the rain are shaken dry
By the whisper of the Gardener in White.

This Coming Winter

This coming winter I will say goodbye –
In case I do not live to see the spring –
To all my loved ones one by one. That way,
Taking my time each time, I need not be
Besieged at the last hour, with the fine thing
Eluding me that I wished to convey
To each face, always granted I could tell
Which one was which as they, around my bed,
Vied not to notice that my mouth no more
Could shape the easy phrase. Nothing said well
To suit the occasion: mutterings instead,
And then not even those. No, long before
That night I'll call them separately aside
And speak my heart so as to save my pride

From injury when I search for a word
And finally words fail me. All will hear
My fond farewells ahead of time, save one:
Only my granddaughter will not have heard
How sad I am to bow out. Not from fear
Of hurting her will I leave this undone:
My aim is otherwise. I'd like to keep
Her thinking that I'm in some way still there
When she laughs, as we did together when
Basil in all his tallness took a steep
Dive as he rushed behind the counter. Where
Was Manuel? She knew. Basil forgot again!
Miraculous, the way she understood
That how the scene was built made it so good.

Let me be part, then, of her memory
Each time the comedy of life strikes her
As wonderful. In that way to live on
Is my wish, though I'll not be there to see
A single giggle. That my last days were
Lit by her friendship until I was gone
Is not for me to tell her, at her age.
Let any last words that she hears from me
Be about Johnny English and the scene
In which he wrecks the sushi bar. A page
Of my book will turn soon, and it might be
The last, but I would want my death to mean
No more to her than our shared sense of doom
When Basil takes charge of the dining room.

Until that day, and never before then,
Let there be no big talk of what is lost
When one friend stays, the other goes away,
And all their sprightly chat comes to an end.
Think rather of the continuity
Prepared for her if she, in times to come,
At any moment when her heart is light,
Should cast her mind back to these laughing hours
And think me part of them. A tiny part
Will do. She'll have her own concerns.
There must be independence for the heart:
It is by cutting loose that the mind learns,
And therefore, wishing to transfer my powers –
To give her, for her life, the memory
Of how I laughed when she made fun of me –
I shall renounce them at the fall of night
As I move on to find Elysium.

Finch Conference

Known as a charm, the bunch of goldfinches,
Polished so prettily from head to heels,
Do girl-group step routines like the Ronettes.
You would not be astonished if Phil Spector
Showed up by limo to collect the money.

The chaffinch arrives solo like Karsavina
On the first night of *The Firebird* in Paris,
When no one credited her speed on stage.
If she would just stay still, that russet bodice
Would look like satin dyed and draped by Bakst.

After her triumph, in the dressing room,
The new star, sitting down to darn her tights,
Was told that from now on she didn't have to.
"It was then," she wrote later in her memoirs,
"That I realised I was Karsavina."

It's getting late. The garden has gone quiet.
The conference of the finches is dismissed.
Time to go in and rest from too much watching
How time, like fame, flies on such fleeting wings.
No birds were hurt in the making of this poem.

The Rest is Silence

or

Stroking Her Feet to Opus 131

I

Rehearsing this quartet, Beethoven heard
Nothing at all. He checked the players by
Watching their bows. He barked the odd harsh word
But couldn't hear that either, and yet I
Am blissed out once again by what he found
When searching in his world without a sound
There, near the end. The Ninth was done. To die

Was really all the man had left to do,
And yet he did this. In our time apart,
Grand opera was what most appealed to you,
But now I hope that you may take to heart
This music without voices, which in fact
Is singing in its essence, the contact
Of Earth with Heaven in a surf of art

Whose forms diversify and fractionate
Past all our expectations except one:
What happens next will be well worth the wait
And prove a burst of beauty was begun
Far back, the way the upsurge of the sun
Is written in the stars.

II

I love this bit, this bit I love. Bit this,
Bit that. Fragments advance. Collect. Go back.
These pizzicato figures you can fit
Short words of Shakespeare to. Alas, alack,
To smooth. That rough. Touch with. A tender kiss.
Enough of that. This is the end of it.
Too smooth. Examine that word "soothe":
It's so, oh, *the*. The flexing female foot,
Touched underneath by a male fingernail,
Signals approval of a cruel finesse.
Suave harshness. Harshly suave. Again. Stop go.
Of that which is desired, too much.
Of that which is desired too much, no end.
But soft, she stirs. Be not at fault. Go slow.
A cliff of dissonance grinds to a halt
And turns to snowflakes on a windless night
That fall past the streetlight.

III

The end was coming in his quiet kingdom.
A tyrant with his conversation books
Which really meant that he did all the talking,
He set old friends against each other. He
Was never a nice man as Haydn was.
I know you think I cite the bastardry
Of artists to excuse myself because
My conscience would ache otherwise. It's true,
But let me say – I'll whisper it – this much:
It might have taken inner turmoil to

Bring him at last to this sublimity,
A fist of rage unfolding to a touch
As light as fingertips on curling toes,
And if he did not smile, watching the bows,
It meant a blessing when he did not frown.
Still air, still air, and still the flakes come down.

IV

The women he loved best were out of reach –
The Countess Kegelwicz, Countess Guicciardi,
Countess Erdödy, Countess This or That –
Because of his low birth. Pity him, then:
His "van" did not mean "von". He was not noble,
Except for ranking above any man
Alive, and she, the one he called Immortal,
The Immortal Beloved,
Knew that, and gave him what she had to give:
They kissed each other, at the very least.
"My angel, my everything, my very self"
He wrote, and wrote it always in his music.
His Josephine was like Napoleon's: there always
Even under other names. Jeanette,
Eleanore, Magdelena and Babette:
They all were her, and when he reached for her
They all were in his arms. Born for each other.
Sie waren für einander geboren
Wrote her sister Therese. Unless Therese
Was the Immortal Beloved. Speculation
Continues. But for sure, though short and ugly,
The famously great flirt was not all talk:
He knew exactly what a woman felt like,

Although, perhaps, it only almost happened.
The Distant Beloved was someone else again,
And no one has an inkling who Elise was –
We just know he wrote her a bagatelle
Which, played on YouTube by Pogorelich,
Must stir the depths of his immobile hairstyle –
But it's fair to guess Beethoven felt the heat
A woman gives off even from her insteps,
Before he reached the cool room of these structures
Separately drifting in transparent air,
Connected only by the space between them.

V

For just a few bars you can hear the fury
With which he crossed the Emperor's name
Off the *Eroica*. If you first have that,
Then later Florestan and Leonore
Can come back to each other's arms.
It's said of him he wrote only one opera
And yet he wrote the only opera,
But here, too, we are listening to voices:
It's just that they've been turned to wood and catgut
Like metamorphoses from Ovid.
Out of the tumult drifts serenity
All the more calm from being so hard-won:
Sweetness from bitterness, a prisoner
Released into the sunlight.

VI

As from the white break of the vault there slides
The surf rider
Trailing his seaside fingertips
Like a stylus through the wave's green face,
Out of the conflict a new concord comes
With an extra grace,
A bride's glide,
Like the peaceful grief on the Madonna's lips
Of the St Peter's Pietà.
It's sixty years since I first heard the Seventh
And knew I would write poetry for life,
And we, for all that time, have known each other,
And for most of it been man and wife,
And, now it has been proved not even I
Could quite destroy all that,
We are still here, together for as long
As life permits. Next stop, eternity:
Which could be what he's trying to say now.

VII

Did he know his death was close? No one can tell.
He might have thought it had already come
When deafness did. This loveliness might sound
Like a summation, but we should beware
Of teleology. He left a sketch
For a Tenth symphony. Art masters have
Rarely packed up to leave the studio:
They live in it, and always would do more.
Though they might turn their faces to the wall,

They sing in silence. After this last note
Silence returns, but is not the same void
We heard before the start. In silence squared
We rise up from the couch and live again,
As if on the first day we ever touched.

Edith Piaf on YouTube

Nobody sings a song of love like her.
I've picked three tracks you haven't heard before
To take us back again to where we were
When we first met.
Tu es partout. Je sais comment. La valse de l'amour.

If we had heard these then, would we have been
So bold as to believe love might stay true?
She says that love has nothing it can mean
Beyond its loss.
La valse de l'amour. Je suis content. Tu es partout.

The long run happened and we placed the bet.
We rolled the dice and saw them pitch and toss,
And still it seems we're no more finished yet
Than these songs are:
La vie en rose. Ah! Ça ira! Ne me quitte pas.

A Heritage of Trumpets

The clear, clean line was always the ideal.
Though there was subtlety in how Miles muttered,
One always ached to hear a song-line uttered
With definition, lyrical and real:
A well-timed silence puncturing the swing
Only to add propulsion. Play that thing!

Bunk Johnson used to do that, way back when,
Inheriting the clean articulation
Of Buddy Bolden. The controlled sensation
Of vaulting gold that drove a funeral then,
Linked death to dancing people, grief to joy:
The rich, sweet notes rang like the real McCoy.

The open horn was king. There was no mute,
Not even Cootie's, that could set the measure
Of confidently opened casks of treasure
Lighting the cave, and turning the blue suit
Of tactful mourning to a pirate kit:
The lawlessness, the skipping lilt of it.

Pure gold in Paris after WWII,
Bill Coleman's open horn proved mainstream muscle
Could still outstrip the nervous, shuffling hustle
Of New York be-bop. Louis Armstrong blew
Coherent lines until the very end.
The same requirement applies, my friend,

To you, and all the more so as the day
Arrives when silence reigns, and Bix in glory
With just one passing phrase sums up your story:
The dying voice of silence. Blaze away
Into the dark, bugler. Be sure the night
Reflects your song with every point of light.

Panis Angelicus

Tipped off by you, I watched the YouTube clip
Of Pavarotti and his father singing
That transcendental César Franck duet
In the gallery of Modena Cathedral.
Slowly the lens pans up, and there they are.

Now they are in my dreams, perhaps because
The guiding father is a theme for me
That aches a long way down. More likely, though,
This haunting happens for the simple reason
They sound so very beautiful together

We might be listening to a strand of life
Slowly assembling and made audible
In all its linkages and balancings,
As if the way an angel sings had been
Caught in a mirror and returned through time.

A lifetime has gone by since we first listened
To music and, wrapped in it, found each other.
Forgive me for not seeing straight away
It was the blessing by which we two pagans
Late in our lives might eat the bread of angels.

Sweet Disaster

(Ronsard Sings of Hélène)

For you, it's easy to lay down the law
At your age, just a fraction of my age.
All you need do is turn another page
And suddenly you see my name no more.
Where have I gone? It's almost a surprise,
But all too soon you will believe your eyes

And think I vanished, as you told me to,
From all the world. The world, though, is still here
For me, and achingly devoid of you –
Worse, there are fantasies that come too near
Resembling you. They bend and speak to me
In your voice, whispering, "What do you see?"

I see you sighing in the grip of bliss:
That much you heard me say, and now you say
Well, that will do. No more for you today,
Or ever. Not a touch and not a kiss.
I have my life to start. This has to end
With one clean break that no soft soap can mend.

Bravely I take it in and hope you lie,
But know you don't, for you are not the type:
Too true by nature. When you caught my eye
I knew already that our time was ripe
To run its course in just a year or less
And end. And now I live with my distress

And it is worse, far worse, than I supposed
It might be when I first became aware
That I would suffer if you were not there.
I still can't bear to see the chapter closed,
And it is months now and will soon be years
That you are not here to behold my tears.

What was achieved? For you, I hope and trust,
Some guarantee there is a gentle touch
A man can have which proves him not unjust
In this dispute where women risk so much:
And as for me, although I lost, I won
Your love awhile, a great thing to have done.

Throughout this poem I have changed the frame
To bring two rhymes together, then apart,
Thus echoing, with one cry from my heart,
Our dance of love. Let this, then, be your fame
When you are gone, if it be my fame too,
To find true glory through my loss of you.

Declaration of Intent

My poems are the balladry of cavaliers
Composed in the lost cause that was the King's,
And if from time to time their ink seems blurred with tears
It is because the way of things
Has gone against the haughty confidence
That once allied sweet music to sound sense,
So now their rhymes and rhythms count as frills and rings.

My poems are the closing words of heretics
Burnt to a cinder and their dust dispersed.
A fierce belief that melts to stain the courtyard bricks
Proves its sincerity at first,
But fades in sunlight as the winning side
Writes history and denies even the pride
Of those who lost, the cruelty that hurts them worst.

My poems written now that I must take my leave
Give thanks good fortune saw me kindly borne
To this departure point, and therefore when they grieve
It is for anyone they mourn
But me. I still recall, when I'm alone,
Children of my age marked with stars and thrown
Into the night and fog, the falling ash of dawn.

My poems sing of life. Though death is also there
In how they crystallise an emphasis
Like a tango maestro pausing, they do not despair:
They just acknowledge the abyss
Awaiting us. It brings finality
To what we were. It will do that for me
Soon now. My poems prove that I accepted this.

My poems take defeat for granted, but they say,
Gallant or gaunt, if we can choose to die
We have been blessed to live. It never came my way,
That random flail of chance, and why
My life must end is known to me. In view
Of these facts, I take care that what I do
Pays back the luck with which I lived to see time fly.

Initial Outlay

I take off my disguise and thus reveal
The man I used to be but now am not.
Surely when I made mirth I was less real
Than I am now. Before this thing I've got
Made laughter hard, I used to spread around
My sunny nature with a liberal hand:
Not overdoing it, you understand,
But eager to amuse, if not astound.

My death came very near, and out of that
I also tried to make a joke, but then
Death didn't happen and the joke fell flat,
And bit by bit I came alive again.
I still faced doom, but when that day would be
Was back in question. Thus I shared the case
Of anyone at all, since all must face
That imprecisely distant certainty.

Winter again, but low on snow and ice.
My lungs are less taxed than they might have been.
The distant thunder of the rolling dice
Grows silent, as if death had quit the scene.
At this rate I will still be here in spring,
And that will make, since I fell ill, six years
I wasn't meant to have. I could shed tears
For what I've lost, but I've gained everything:

My family built this house for me just so
That I may read and write. No doubt my last
Lines will be written here. For all I know,

That means tomorrow, but for now the past,
So vivid in my mind, suggests I might
Consider both men real, the cock-a-hoop
Rapscallion and this old crock with the stoop
Who sits and scrawls away the live-long night,

Making a neat design of penitence,
Transmuting shame into a melody,
As if the senseless paved the way for sense
Or craft made up for infidelity,
And all that heartbreak were the price for this
That I at last can do now, having learned
The truth about the cost for all concerned
Of my apprenticeship in artifice.

Night-Walker's Song

How strange, that now my strength is sunk so low,
My powers of handicraft have reached their height,
Starting new poems even in the night
So I must, cursing, rise, and slowly go
Downstairs to settle at my desk and write
Until my kitchen fills with the dawn light,
And pages fill, too, with fresh stanza frames
I fancy rich and sweet as honeycomb,
Black holes on paper where starlight, instead
Of hiding, comes back sparkling from the dead.
Why don't I think that these are just word-games
A broken man plays in the nursing home?
What if this upsurge is a weakness too,
The last flare of a fever overdue
To break these many years? But surely not:
Look at the park parade of what I've said –
A Chinese opera among table-tops,
The Russian Ballet and the Keystone Kops,
The dust of diamonds from a pepper pot,
Colours and metals out of Camelot –
And envy me as I trudge back to bed.
A whole new day is here, and still I live
To strut my stuff, give what I have to give.
Though it might not be much, it is my best
And while it comes to me I know no rest,
But must be at it, threading syllables,
Timing the wind chimes, balancing the bells,
Until each line reveals the harmony
Of its creation by destroying me:
Always my fate, still my imperative.

I serve the joy-spring of the language. Let
Me pass, therefore. I am not finished yet.
I merely need to sleep awhile, and then,
Perhaps before nightfall, begin again.

Final Reminder

Reading Laforgue, I love the way he crowds
The world of things into his racing frame
Yet makes them fit, like lightning in the clouds.
The toads, the vermin get their blaze of fame
In his high-speed, grab-bag democracy
Of thought, perception and the sheer desire
To live. Each stanza, as if meant for me,
Spits like an ember of his funeral pyre
Sculpted into a message of reproof
For any moment that I doubt the worth
Of effort, any wish to stand aloof
At long last from the turmoil of the Earth
Now my light fades. The stars are on display
In the dark night, not the bright sky of day.

Carpentry of the Quatrain

A four-square stanza is the magic box
Neat thoughts fit into and combine their glow
Into a furnace. Lucky the lid locks,
Or we'd see ashes fluttering like snow.

Given the chance I'd work no other way,
But there are ideas that refuse to fit,
The thought that needs more space to have its say
No matter how severe you are with it.

But even then, the best way to contain
The sprawl is to remember, flying blind,
Your ideal of the right cup for the rain.
With nothing spilled and everything designed,

Wish and fulfilment click, the whirlpool swirls
And freezes, and it's there before your eyes:
The cubic lattice of selected pearls
Stacked rim to rim, the orderly surprise.

Head Wound

The carcinoma left a bullet hole
High on my forehead. It looked like a tap
By a pro hit-man. In fact the killer's role
Was played not by a pistol-toting chap
But by a pretty female whose light touch
Sliced out the blob and pieced a flap of skin
Into the gap. It didn't hurt that much.
When finally the pit was all filled in
A pink *yarmulke* of Elastoplast
Topped off the job. The whole thing happened fast.

The wound, alas, healed slowly, but the heap
Of duct-tape mercifully was replaced
By one neat bandage, though I had to keep
Changing it each second day. I faced
At least three weeks of wearing this square patch
And there were interviews for my new book
Demanding to be done. A tale to match
My rather daring James Bond sort of look
Seemed called for, so I mentioned MI5,
A mild gun battle. I got out alive.

No sooner did the first show go to air,
A dear old lady stopped me in the street
And said I really ought to take more care
In gun fights. I thought her a shambling dunce
But only for a moment. All the fault
Had been mine, for expecting that my smirk
Would flag the gag. Alas, there is a rule:
The straight-faced joke that might work on the page
Is death on TV. I should act my age.

Candy Windows

He runs in slo-mo with a wall of flame
Boiling behind him like Valhalla's fall
In *Götterdämmerung*. He made his name
From being bullet-proof. He summons all
His skills to get the girl from Bucharest
To Rome or Paris or wherever suits
The budget. Somewhere she can get undressed:
The only scene for which we give two hoots.
The heavies blast the road or bomb the train.
The dialogue is dreck, the plot inane.

They make love. Breasts and bottoms fill the frame
When suddenly the whole motel explodes:
The bad guys in a tank. Devoid of shame,
He frisks her lovely corpse for the launch codes
Of the secret anthrax time-bomb missile thing.
They're tattooed on her thigh. But look, she stirs.
The soundtrack fills with strings that soar and sing.
When has he ever seen a face like hers
Since his last movie? He, the Teflon star
Scoops up the jail-bait and runs for the car.

The enemy is an army: all the same
He kills the lot, but finds himself alone.
The girl is gone, and gradually the game
Changes. He fails to steal the new nose-cone
His HQ wants, and where once he could burst
Through candy windows, now he fears they might
Be real glass, and – much worse, the very worst –
The gathering night could really be the night
When he, immortal once, but not again,
Must bruise and bleed and die like other men.

Elephant in the Room

On slow last legs it comes to the right spot
Near the dried-up river bed where it may kneel
And die. The plain is open, with one clump of trees
Parched, bleached, more grey than green,
Much like the grass:
The perfect setting for what happens next.

What happens next is nothing. Still upright,
Precisely balanced on its bended knees,
The elephant decays. All by itself
It loses its last flesh with neither vultures
Nor hyenas to help with the unloading:
They seem to have been paid to stay away.

When all the meat is gone
There is only skin, draped thickly on its cage
Of bones. Perhaps the ants are in there
Like vagrants in the ruins of New York.
There might be termites cleaning out its tusks.
If so, it shows no signs of pain or anger.

Through hollow eyes it looks out of the screen
With what seems an inflexible resolve.
The shadow of its former self has timed
Its exit to sum up what it did best,
To bulk large as a thing of consequence
Even though emptied of its history.

A breath of wind will knock it down, an hour
Of rain wash it away, but until then,
Sustained by stillness, it is what it is:
A presence, a whole area in space
Transformed into a single living thing
That now, its time exhausted, lives no more.

Quiet Passenger

When there is no more dying left to do
And I am burned and poured into a jar,
Then I will leave this land that I came to
So long ago, and, having come so far,
Head home to where my life's work was begun.
But nothing of that last flight will I see
As I ride through the night into the sun:
No stars, no ocean, not the ochre earth,
No patterns of dried water nor the light
That streams into the city of my birth,
The harbour waiting to take down my dust.
So why, in that case, should I choose to go?
My day is done. I go because I must:
Silence will be my way of saying so.

In Your Own Time

Ridi, Pagliaccio

Back to the gate, back to the lounge, back to
The shuttle bus, the same airport hotel,
This flight continues to go nowhere. You
Long ago realised that you would do well
Not to complain at one more wasted day:
The flight is going nowhere anyway,

And there is nothing wasted as you learn –
Almost as if life had begun again –
To use the time, to read, to write, to earn
Your keep. That you are frail like other men
Is now proved, with a force that even you
Can't laugh off. What we are is what we do.

Back, then, to what you do best. Give a thought
The curve of words that makes a wing of it.
Get one more line to sing the way it ought.
Anything well expressed is holy writ:
Your occupation, even now, when time
Is almost gone, is honest. It's no crime

To spend these stolen hours as if your fate
Depended on the balance of a phrase.
It always did, and even now, so late,
As your pen feels its way through the word maze,
The thrill of getting things exactly right
Prepares you for the long flight through the night.

The Back of My Hand

I used to know the back of my hand
Like the back of my hand
But things are happening now that I can't
Quite, in my mind, command
To make sense of themselves.

On the smooth plateau from the root
Of the index finger
To the thumb joint where a light plane
Without the slightest danger
Could once have glided in for a dead-stick landing
There are bumps that would stop a truck.
It's all so demanding,

This ageing business. It starts with
The simple exaggeration
Of veins making tracks like the river system
Of a whole new nation
Suddenly put in place by the Space Invaders,
The flyers from Atrophon
Who built all this stuff and then died out.
And now they are gone,

And the ruins of whoever saw them off
Are being overtaken
By other ruins: the product,
Unless I'm very much mistaken,
Of a people wedded to chaos
In the first instance,
Who keep what they take and cover it

With a carpet of decrepitude.
I was proud of these hands once.

Now I don't even care to look.
It would be like sitting in a canvas
Chair at Angkor Wat
To watch the jungle taking back
That elegant structure
While some expert gave me a personal lecture.
Or do I mean Oaxaca? Carlos Fuentes told me
That was the place to see. In his last years
Did the backs of his hands still say "hold me"
To all those women who loved his eyes?

At least I have a voice,
Or I did until I started the new tablets.
But no one has a real choice
We have to take what's given to us,
Especially in here
While the campfires of the onslaught
Draw nearer every night
To this place that I know by now
Like the back of my hand.
Take a look if you like. You know what this is?
It's the Promised Land.

Ibrutinib

The Marvel Comic name should tip you off
That this new drug is heavy duty stuff.
You don't get this one just to cure a cough.
A chemo pill, and powerful enough
To put the kibosh on your CLL,
It gets in there and gives the bastard hell.

Five years' remission and the beast is back.
It's in your bones the way the Viet Cong
Poured through their tunnels to the Tet attack,
And what comes next might not last very long.
But let's see what Ibrutinib can do
To win the war whose battlefield is you.

Ibrutinib, you little cluster-bomb
Of goodness, get in there and do your thing!
All that the bad guys seek is martyrdom:
Their own demise is in the death they bring.
They work in cells. There is no high command.
We drop you in and then it's hand to hand.

Should you prevail, we promise you a role
From here on in until the natural end.
Just beat them back and it will be a stroll,
Unless you don't, in which case things might tend
To go bananas in a serious way.
But not yet. Down the hatch. This is today.

Side Effects of Medication

I feel dull from the blue pill that I took,
Notoriously a flattener of mood.
I triple-read each sentence of my book
And by slow-loping furies am pursued;

Except they never reach me. Just their wheeze
And whine and whistle irritate my ear.
A Tiger tank is hidden in the trees:
Time's chariot broods on ways to hurry near.

A whir, a blur, a whingeing void in flight,
Shaped flame eats into me and halves my weight.
The muscles in my legs are pipe-clay tight.
Time for another pill. It must be late:

It must be later than I think, I think.
Another dose of Nothing Done begins,
And there is lemon squash for us to drink.
May Christ forgive me for the worst of sins,

The one the old-style monks called accidie.
It meant to have an ice-field for a face.
I shave myself. I that knew ecstasy
Cope with the clean-up of my fall from grace,

And start another day on the inside.
I try to write. The pieces will not fit
Together. In the phrase "broke down and cried"
Note what comes first. There is no end to it.

Not Forgetting George Russell

How funny, in the sense of not being funny,
It ought to be that here, on the nut farm –
A Cambridge feature Rupert Brooke left out
For obvious reasons –
In a cool morning when all except the nurses
Are tranked out of their skulls,
I haunt the kitchen reading an old essay,
Trying to find my tone again –
The one about Ernst Robert Curtius,
The only modern scholar you called great –
In praise of Dante's long love for his teacher.
You were Brunetto and I . . . Well, let that pass,
Though we, of course, were butch as panther sweat.

Ten years ago, when you were still alive
If only just, we met for one last time
When I came out to get my Hodgins medal,
The literary gong that I most prize.
It's only justice if Les cops the Nobel,
Don't you agree? They say the A380
Airbus was built for getting him to Stockholm.
When he gets given it, it might do something
To tame our literati's national sense
Of isolation that you found so foolish:
You that inhabited no other boundaries
Save those of Christendom.

From Adelaide I day-tripped to Mildura
And then by car out to Cullulleraine,
A six-house town parked in the open mulga

Where, in an easy chair on the veranda,
You lay with cling-film skin, and Isobel
Controlled the cakes: "Another Lamington?"
"There can't be more," I said. "The world supply
Is here," you whispered. Loving to be teased,
She knew that these jokes might well be the last,
As you, the master of the *ars moriendi*,
Took in, with ruined lungs, just enough air
To prove you could still smile.

"Waste no time saying what need not be said"
Was what you'd taught me, but I had a plan:
A subtle plan for doing Dante over
In English. But you had enough to cope with
Just being proud of my wife, rising star
Of the Società Dantesca,
A ruthless *cosa nostra*. The prettiest
Of all your brilliant creatures had to shoot
Her way into that place and wade in blood.

I'm sure she told you, loving you as always,
When she came out to see you. But it's time
For my Caped Hero to come bursting forth:
I, Dante, Flash of Lightning! At a cinema
Near you! I wonder if there is one. Never mind:
Books need no screens. This fanfare is a token
Of how I valued all the times we spoke:
Something to leave with you as I now leave you,
The same way you invariably left us
With some new thrill to chase up: Hindemith,
Matisse, Stravinsky . . . any works that burn
The brain like that are works of God, you said:
They speak of what He lost. And now at last

So say I, weeping, by my tears made blind,
As the nurse comes with her cup of colours
And your thin outline melts into the smoke.

—Addenbrooke's Hospital, Cambridge, UK, July 1, 2011

Imminent Catastrophe

The imminent catastrophe goes on
Not showing many signs of happening.
The ice at the North Pole that should be gone
By now, is awkwardly still lingering,

And though sometimes the weather is extreme
It seems no more so than when we were young
Who soon will hear no more of this grim theme
Reiterated in the special tongue

Of manufactured fright. Sea Level Rise
Will be here soon and could do such-and-such,
Say tenured pundits with unblinking eyes.
Continuing to not go up by much,

The sea supports the sceptics, but they, too,
Lapse into oratory when they predict
The sure collapse of the alarmist view
Like a house of cards, for they could not have picked

A metaphor less suited to their wish.
A house of cards subsides with just a sigh
And all the cards are still there. Feverish
Talk of apocalypse might, by and by,

Die down, but the deep anguish will persist:
His own death, not the Earth's, is the true fear
That motivates the doomsday fantasist:
There can be no world if he is not here.

Splinters from Shakespeare

My name is Shallow. Lend me credit, pray,
If I, at this stage, sound deep once or twice.
They called me "lusty Shallow" in my day,
But time ensured that I would pay the price,
Which is to wonder where my juices went.
Jesu, the mad, mad days that I have spent.

My cousin Silence would attest, were he
To find a voice, I left no woman cold.
This poor forked radish once was a green tree,
And now I hear Jane Nightwork has grown old
Who said she spurned me, but that was not true.
The death I owe to God has fallen due.

I heard the chimes at midnight with Sir John,
But he was stirring, even as he sighed.
He sucked up his great sack-butt and moved on,
And left me here alone to nurse my pride.
I, too, have lived: a small life, but not mean.
Jesu, Jesu, the days that I have seen.

Lee Miller in Hitler's Bathtub

But if you didn't know, you'd never guess
Whose bath it was. You'd see only the woman,
So beautiful that since the time of Helen
She's started wars, the perennial temptress,

But abstract nonetheless. You have to know her:
Picasso's friend, an angel of adventure.
Sheer daring brought her sweet skin to this juncture
With porcelain that would look dull without her,

But not be famous now except the other
Bare bottom that once sat in it was his,
Killer of millions. Remember that this is
Only a footnote. Don't get in a lather:

But while reflecting that a sponge wipes clean
Only so much, do take time to recall
That if this nymph were Leni Riefenstahl
There would be less, not more, for her to mean.

But we are safe, when contemplating this
Unsmiling incandescent odalisque,
From any hint of awe. That was the risk:
To gloss trash with a misplaced emphasis.

But me no buts. Enough to say that Lee
Was not just lovely but sane, smart and good.
By her, his squalor was well understood.
Bless her for throwing light on perfidy.

Sunt lacrimae rerum

There are tears in things. Things mortal touch the heart.
On the *favela*, sitting in the paste
Of clay and urine, in the fever season
At the festering tip of a high-level Hades,
Is the plastic duck of a little girl who died
Of typhus, and the image makes me blink,
Recalling the lost earring found inside
The crumpled dashboard of a crushed Mercedes.

Choral Service from Westminster Abbey

The Abbey choir sings "I Know Not the Hour"
And once again we all sit silent where
She, only, was not sighing for the waste
Of youth, health, beauty and the *savoir faire*
That might have served us all well later on
Had there not been the panic-stricken haste,
The concrete tunnel and the car's crushed power,
Almost as if she wanted to be gone,

Even without a chance to say goodbye.
From my seat on the transept's left-hand aisle
I saw the ceremony end. Six men
Shouldered the coffin and I could have sworn
That they brought her to me. You well might smile,
But *she* could smile as if she were the dawn
All set for a night out. That she would die
So soon, and never race your heart again,

Seemed not in nature. Then the guards wheeled right
A yard in front of me, and their slow march –
Spit-shine parade boots on a flagstone floor –
Down the side corridor beyond the arch
Crunched, boomed and whispered and went silent. So
She started her flight home. It felt like theft.
Until she vanished few of us could know –
And now all knew, and nothing was more sure –

A light could die just from the way it shone.
Her fantasy, or ours? I couldn't say.
She pulled the names, she got them on her team:
No question. Think, though, of some crippled kid
She talked to a long time, and later on
Wrote letters to, and never said she did.
Tell yourself then that she was just a dream,
Gone when the soldiers carried her away.

Ayrton Senna Killed at Imola

Thousands of miles away in Buenos Aires
Juan Manuel Fangio, five times world champion,
Watched Senna hit the Armco and sit still.
The world over, we were all interpreting
The silence. Fangio needed only that first glance
And turned the TV off.
Such stillness was a language,
The signal that the angel had departed.

As I write this now
Schumacher is out walking at his home
On Lake Geneva,
Getting the exercise he just might need
If ever his mind comes back.

Moss when he spun across the grass
At Donington with me beside him looking
As if I had seen my own ghost;
Or Derek Warwick on the *autostrada*
Driving me down to Monza;
Or Alan Jones in that brutal Lamborghini
In Adelaide when we entertained the crowd
With our brilliant imitation of a champion driving
His panic-stricken friend to hospital . . .
But now all these faces are from long ago
And even
When Damon, in my dreams, comes back to drive me
Under police escort to the airport in Hungary,
I can't believe how very young he looks.

Deborah, my elder daughter's friend,
A magnet for adventurous men,
Was taken to a Grand Prix one weekend.
She got so bored she lay down for a sleep
Beside a pile of tyres.
When she woke up again she couldn't see.
Her eyes were full of rain.

Verse Letter

In reply to Ann Baer, aged 101, of Richmond-on-Thames.

Your handwriting, so perfect for its style
And firmness, made me feel that this must be
A brilliant schoolgirl. Hence my knowing smile
At your comparing of my maple tree

With Tennyson's. But further down the page,
And seemingly in passing, you revealed
The secret of your learning: your great age.
In your day, verse was not a special field,

It was a language, so to speak: a tongue
For all who read books. No such luck today,
Alas. Just look at how it keeps you young,
This love for words that time can't take away

From anyone touched with it early on.
No wonder that you write a hand so fair.
I swear that you'll be here when I am gone,
Just as my fiery tree will still be there –

Bathed in its poetry, the rain, the air.

Aldeburgh Dawn

I

From slate sea that would gleam white were it not
The Gulf Stream cooled by nothing except England,
A run-down sun emerges to remind me
How far it came last night from where it always
Behaves as if it had never been to Europe
And burns your cheeks. This version chills them stiff.
The light is thin, even the wind is thin –
The strain of love as sung by Peter Pears –
And on the roofs of cars that shone before
Under the lamps but now are lit from space,
Those tears are not the dew of the Pacific,
Just drops of rain.
                              Three quarters of the poets
Here at the Festival speak double Dutch
From where I stand, still stuck with rhyme and rhythm.
This isn't Edinburgh or Cheltenham:
It's more like, well, a modest out-of-town
Gig with the smell of fish thrown in. You read,
Take questions, sign your books and hit the sack.
In charge, the fine young lady with the eyes –
Toast Catalogue meets *Poetry* (Chicago) –
Will spark a poem from the chap who looks
Like the top half of Ted Hughes, but that's the lot,
Unless you clock the haddock they bring in
On toy boats with no names but only numbers,
To fill the crunchy gold beer-batter sleeves
In the restaurant your hotel is famous for.

II

But look, you must have done well. On the second
Pale morning when the same dawn walks again,
Poseidon, with his Maserati logo
Wrapped to the barbs in kelp and bladderwrack,
Comes bubbling up and shouts to you: "Good choice!
I make this scene at least one day a year.
You have to keep it real sometimes, and I
Get tired of Acapulco and the Hamptons.
Too many big yachts I can't tower over.
Too many Russian girls. Too much Ralph Lauren.
Bling eats the soul."
                              His beard, indeed, I note,
As well as all the standard shells and pearls,
Has plastic bags in it. What better warrant
For throttling back on pretty talk? And if
I can't do that, what am I doing here,
Watching the nun-like progress of Aurora?
She bends to touch the ever-shifting shingle,
Her grey-on-grey cloak pink just at the edges,
And breathes cold light on salt-cured wildflowers –
Small, pinched, set wide apart. Lives of the poets.

III

The sun is up, the low clouds drained away
From the horizon, and beside the shell
Rigged on the beach as if for selling petrol
To veteran Ducks that got lost after D-Day,
I scan the flat sea and the pale blue vault
Streaked at the far edge with the vapour trails

Of the morning's first jets racing into Holland.
This fan of metal Maggi Hambling built,
Apparently from concentrated rust,
Is hard edged, two men high, and takes the sun
No better than a half-track opened up
By a Typhoon's rocket in the Falaise Gap,
But the rubric at its rim shines clear and bright:
"I hear those voices that will not be drowned."
Words meant to make us think of *Peter Grimes*,
But I think of the *Deutschland* and the festivals
That Hopkins never went to. Pagan gods
Are all I see where he saw Christ in glory:
A matching shell, but this time luminous,
Awash with lustre, rises from the water,
And Venus speaks.
                              "I'm stunned that you can face me.
When have you ever suffered for your art?
Men who weren't mad for glamour gave their lives
To work here. You should try it for ten minutes."
The men she meant, of course, were Britten's crew:
Abbots of music I enjoy so little
I long for an old world put back together
So Erich Wolfgang Korngold might have written
A lot more operas. I made that much clear,
Yet still she lay down on the rug I'd brought,
Saying she didn't feel the cold. I did:
I kept my clothes on and just looked at her,
Trying to tell myself it was enough
To see her, since the memory would serve,
And she need not appear to me again –
Not her nor any of the other gods
I stole from Bullfinch back in the year dot.
One last kiss, then. Roll up the empty rug,

And back to the hotel across the pebbles,
So far from the hot sand that formed my habit
Of softening reality with dreams.
High time, I thought, for putting paid to that:
If I see revenants, then they should come
From the latest burned-out girls' school in the Valley
Of Swat, be cursed with sense enough to see
That this place – silent, bleak, so short of action
You can hear the lichen grow – is next to heaven.

IV

The second and last night, my main event:
On stage to talk about my favourite poems
By everyone but me. Points of technique.
(Nothing is catchier than talking shop.)
The audience has copies. I point out
Frost's "Silken Tent" is put together like
Its subject – all the tensions are resolved,
Simply by balance, into relaxation –
While Larkin knows there is no sanctuary.
By which of them is beauty more hard-won?
Scanning the crowded hall, I duly note
That the top half of Ted Hughes is moving in
On the ash blonde with the Téa Leoni profile:
A legend now throughout the festival
For never having heard of Andrew Marvell.
There was a day – like, yesterday – when I
Would have cast her as Helen's sister Phoebe,
The thoughtful one with the career-girl glasses
And a killing line in loose La Perla smalls,
But now my gaze is drawn to a young woman

Distinguished only by her concentration
As she takes notes. Later, I ask her why.
A schoolteacher, no vamp, except her eyes
Burn with her love of poetry, as if
It loved her in its turn. So what we said
Might have a further life beyond our time:
One quoted phrase, one line, one anecdote –
The only immortality that lasts.
No god for that save Mercury, the messenger.

V

Later, near midnight, on the esplanade,
A pair of ancient people hand in hand
Sit on a bench. Ideally they should be
The ghosts of Vishnevskaya and Rostropovitch,
Once happy to make music here. But no,
They're real. "We liked that one about the tent."
Feeling my age, I go back to my room,
Make tea, and catch a re-run of *The Wire*.

Too Many Poets

Too many poets pack a line with thought
But melody refuses to take wing.
It's not that meaning has been dearly bought:
It has been stifled, by a hankering
For portent, as if music meant too much.
Sidney called this a *want of inward touch.*

True poets should walk singing as they weep,
As Arnaut Daniel once epitomised;
But nothing written will be worth its keep
Composed by one who has not realised
This to be true, and tested his own song
On others, seeing if they listen long

Or turn away. Verse is a public act
To that extent at least. As cruel as love,
The wished-for gift declines to be a fact
Except for the elect. The gods above
Loll on their clouds and lazily look down
To choose who gets the laurels of renown

Even if deaf. For them, it's just a game,
But not for us, and though there might well be
Too many poets, we all nurse the same
Faith in the virtue of our mystery.
Courage, my friend: the world will not forget
What you have written. Or at least not yet.

Apotheosis at the Signing Table

Looking ahead for places to sit down,
Come spring I might, one last time, limp downtown
And into Heffers, into Waterstones,
In either order, haul my creaking bones,
To stand, with a long-practised half-lost look,
Somewhere beside the stack of my new book
Until I'm asked to sign. As if surprised
I'll sit down, slowly, seeming paralysed
By sheer humility as they bring stock
Of books that I forgot I wrote. I'll sign
Each tempting title-page with my by-line
Like a machine for hours on end. The clock
Will seem not to exist. My signature
Will grow, however, steadily less sure,
Until, the felt-tip quivering in my grasp,
I scrawl the hieroglyphs of my last gasp.
A final short sip from my cup of tea
And I will topple, croaking tragically.
Slumped on the carpet, I will look around,
And all the walls of books in the background,
More splendid even than they were before,
Will seem to hear my small voice from the floor.
"Heffers or Waterstones, this is goodbye,
But I rejoice that I came here to die,
So one day those who know my books may say
That this is where he signed his life away."

Recollected in Tranquillity

You realise that this is no reprieve
But merely a delay?
The comedy must end. The way it ends
Has just been put off to another day.
Perhaps two months from now, perhaps two years,
It will be known to family and friends
That you, at last, are more dead than alive,
With nothing left to say.
When any tears there are will be their tears,
Not yours, the wave of silence will arrive
With which you leave.

So this must be the storm before the lull,
These webs of words
Slowly assembled at the summer's peak
Here in the portico of your downfall,
As you sit watchfully to count the birds –
So few beside the Heathrow rush of spring –
Which in the garden briefly peck and preen
Before continuing
To Finland, Iceland, Baffin Land, wherever:
Your chance to speak before you never speak
Again, your next to final scene.

This peace, which will be perfect by and by,
Came out of chaos. When the drugs went wrong
It almost seemed a burden not to die
As I shared that Babelic rumpus room
With the trouser thief and the lady with one song
She sang forever. Racing, my brain teemed

With stuff to tell the doctors so they might
Unbolt the door, but that place was a tomb
Sealed tight. I ate my sleeping pills and dreamed
Of all I could have had –

The happiness I wasted. Now, set free,
I see that my whole life
Had been a greedy fever. A sad spell
Of frenzy only summed it up. My wife
And daughters built this studio for me
In which I read and write and rest. They know
Something ill-mended in my mind demands
I live alone. And so they come and go
To help me do that, and so all is well,
As I wait for the day the last bird lands
And nightfall finally

Blankets my vision of this bright arcade.
Outside, in that cane chair,
I sat to read *The Faerie Queene* and found
Garbled accounts of knights and damsels made
Melodic sense, in verse as light as air.
On this desk, crowded as a burial mound
With treasured papers, my Chinese notebook,
Full of unfinished thoughts, will still be there,
When I, at last, can't reach it. Should things look
As if I knew despair, of this be sure:
I loved it here.

The Dark Roses

The roses that I sent on Mother's Day
Maintained, in their glass vase, an after-glow
Of crimson lustre, but their late display
Of faded glory finally was gone
For good. Strange that the shape of every bloom
Remains, the outline of its folds more clear
Now than before. This I must dwell upon:
Here in the sunlight of this perfect room
These roses die well, though they bring night near –
For the darkness in their petals seeks me too,
And once inside it I won't even know
How beautifully designed they are, how true
To life. But for the moment they are here
Where I can see them, as I pray that you
Will think of what I once was when I go:
Not beautiful, as these dead things are still,
But still too full of life for time to kill.

Summer Surprised Us

Supposing this is my last summer, let
What I see here, in all its glory, seem,
Come winter, splendid to my fading gaze
As it is now. Curse me if I forget
The luck that still brings me this waking dream
With such a freshness, here in my last days,
I feel that I was born to breathe the air
The rain has just drenched and cooled everywhere.

It needed cooling. Heat does not belong,
Where I lie down now, to the same degree
As it did there, when I had just been born
And started to grow up. It seems plain wrong
To feel my thin supply of energy
Depleted further, even though the dawn
Is such a flood of light it might as well
Be the Pacific sun. Clear as a bell,

Rinsed by this wetly gleaming afternoon,
The light still sparkles undiminished. When
The temperature retreats, as soon it must,
Things might look more like England, and the moon
Seem less a vast night-club for magic men,
Unless the rearrangement of its dust
Is permanent, and nothing from now on
Will cease from being changed or simply gone.

For how to know that these weeks have not been
The first three quarters of my final act
In which, bemused, my judgment quite undone,
I play Malvolio when, scene by scene,
He stumbles to his downfall? Won't that fact –
Though punctuated by the sunset gun –
Not feel like this, a fantasy, with all
These other people in a fiction's thrall?

I'll ask my keen-eyed daughters. Am I here?
Is all this sunlight real? I hear surf boom
As if I, somehow soon, might swim once more.
But no, these waves are only in my ear:
Tricks, like the way the sunlight in this room,
Transposed through time, is light I saw before
And brings with it the young man I once knew
Who took one look and fell in love with you.

As if you were here now and not sky-high
Walking among the pitched roofs of Kashmir,
I long for you to stroll the quarter mile
From your side of the river and drop by,
Just to be asked if I am fading here
In this white stream of fire. Were you to smile,
I'd take that as a no, though I have learned
Richly to see the sky bleached, the air burned.

The truth is that I need no heat to melt
And die the puddled death of the snowman.
I do that from within. My memories
More than suffice to tell me I've been dealt
A fair hand if not better. I began
In light like this, and saw the burning trees
Cut swathes through mountain ranges. Far too small
Back then to really comprehend it all,

I almost do now. It is life, drawn from
The roaring force of nature, even here
In these polite, pampered gardens. If I live
To see again the cold Elysium
Which is the winter's destiny, forgive –
As if it were a figment of the air –
The weakness I show now, if not the way
I thought it strength, back in a heedless day.

At some time or another, it must be
Near in the future now that I shall lose
My last contact with life, and so depart
To leave behind even the memory
Of those cross garters I was proud to choose.
But that absurd confusion spoke my heart:
I sought release in vain, but at the last
It seeks me with success. The die is cast:

This sudden touch of autumn has begun
At last to take the shine off all I see.
A hint of winter will be in the air
As you fly back to us, but if the sun
Should shine at all, it will for you and me,
Blessing us here as first it blessed us there
When real waves roared and how far we would get
Together neither of us knew as yet.

Tactics of the Air Battle

*(In this fantasy, one of the many young aircrew buried
in the American cemetery outside Cambridge grows old
in his home state, and writes to me.)*

No sudden death was quite as quick as when
The enemy came from the front dead straight,
The closing speed six hundred plus, and then
In just one second, from the wings and snout
He sprayed the shells that ripped your flight deck open
And left an aimless wreck, which went straight down,
The waist and turret gunners jumping ship
If they were lucky. In a flank attack
Sometimes the rudder was shot off,
The flight crew keeping just enough control
To turn for England. But with two or more
Engines shut down and leaking so much fuel?
Forget it. Like unpacked smoke-puffs
Lone parachutes continued to appear
For miles on end. Imagine the mad violence
And then the slow admission of junk status
As their hulking power symbol fell apart.
Boys falling from the cold air, looking up,
Saw the undoing of their citadels.
You might ask why, then, the Krauts didn't win.
The answer is, they ran out of trained flyers.
Our fighters cut theirs down at such a rate
Luftwaffe pilots rated Ace if they
Could land: forget about an actual fight.
Only old hands could even get that near.

The younger ones were heading for the wall
Their first trip out. The Mustangs ate them up:
The Mustangs and the Thunderbolts. P-47s
Could go downhill like dump-trucks and come back
Uphill like seagulls. None of the German planes
Could mix it with a Lightning. Their night-fighters
Stayed in the game because the British bombers
Were unprotected. Finally, of course,
Even the night-fighters went up by day,
With all their radar aerials still on them,
Cutting their speed. It was a turkey shoot:
A Ju-88 would last ten minutes.
The jets and rocket planes would certainly
Have made a difference, but they were too few
And far too late to count. I saw one once,
I mean a jet, the 262. It went
Across our nose as fast as you could blink
And rippled as it launched its bunch of missiles
At someone on the far side of the box
From us. Someone I didn't know, thank Christ,
Was all gone in a flash. If that had happened
Ten times in one raid we'd have had to stop,
And send our bombs to Germany by mail.
But all we saw was nothing but the future
Just getting started, and we came home safe.
I got to die of old age, just like you.
Believe me, son, you didn't miss a thing.

The Gods Make Mischief

The pliability of Jupiter
Is easily explained. When Juno pleaded
For Turnus, what she wished seemed granted her
By the great god. But her wish was not needed

To change his mind, which changed itself: the day
Of death for that young man was undecided
As yet, and in the long run Fate would say
When it would be. Her fervour was misguided:

She spoke too soon. My mother spoke too late.
Our God could not postpone her husband's dying.
It was already done. Though God was great,
Deep into hell her cries of grief went flying,

And I began to be what I became,
Doing my level best to seem undaunted:
What use are gods, if Chance is their real name?
The lifelong question by which I was haunted –
Taunted, as if I were the one to blame.

The Smocking Brick

Across twelve thousand miles of land and ocean
I came here to get most of my work done.
Writings that were no more than a mere notion
One day, and for a while were just begun,
Grew out of those few lines to their fruition
As if I were remembering the sun
And surf of my original condition,
When first I saw the shell the silkworm spun

Was like a golden thimble for my mother
As she worked at the smocking brick. No book
Could be so neatly written. Now no other
Memory haunts me like the pains she took
To decorate those tiny frocks. The weather
Has nothing here to match how thunder shook
Our windows, but still, floating like a feather,
Her needle hand, obeying her fixed look,

Would build neat lattices hour after hour.
Now, for her son, the hours grow few, and yet
I might, impelled by that first taste of power,
Write something to pay off an ancient debt
If I sit up till dawn. Down to the wire,
While I can still breathe I will not forget
Networks of silk that glowed with pastel fire
While she stitched through the day until sunset.

It all took time, and time is a wild river
That one day ceases to reflect the sky.
Eventually the spinning coin will shiver,
The rumble as it falls end with a sigh.
When there is honest toil in the endeavour
Piece-work is noble but cannot defy
The night, which will not wait for me forever.
Her work kept us alive, and as I die

I'm certain I will think of the precision
With which she placed the last stitch in a row.
Never until the failing of her vision
Did she cease to prepare her cloth and sew
With her fine thread the rhymed and scanned equation
Of pure expression and punctilio
That made each separate séance an occasion.
But why was she so quiet? Now I know.

I know now that the shadow of non-being
Will visit anyone who does these things
And stay till they are done. All I was seeing
Was somebody arranging offerings
Before an altar, but there is no saying
Which god was served. What grace such worship brings
Is slow to show itself. We just keep praying
Until that rapt moth spreads its perfect wings

And leaves a cracked cocoon to be translated
Into the luscious filament employed
When seeing squares of cotton recreated,
Making another mother overjoyed
At how her child, too young to get excited
By how she looks, in fact a bit annoyed,
Becomes a princess. Suitably requited,
The toiling seamstress profits from the void:

And finally a poem, too, must render
Obeisance to the dark where it can shine
As only one more star, for no defender
Of this art, which I still hope to make mine,
Denies the overstock we're buckling under.
Yet the compulsion lives. Shaping a line
To mark the shock of recollected thunder,
I stitch the lightning into my design

And see again that tireless needle gleaming
As if its contrapuntal play of light
Were part of what was made. If I were dreaming
I would not also see the fruit-bat's flight
So clearly, or the frangipani blooming,
Their shades of butter in plush cusps of white.
But this is real, and now. The breakers booming
Spatter my eyes with salt tears as I write.

Intergalactic Junket

Junkets my mother made would float in space
Like flying saucers, which were all the rage
At that time. They would settle into place
On the kitchen table so a kid my age
Could listen to them hum and watch them glow
Before they disappeared without a trace
Into the chasm of a childish face,
A throat whose flattered gullet felt the flow.

Sprinkled with nutmeg from beyond the stars
The junket sat there tremulous in its plate
And yet unmoving. Visiting milk bars
When I was still too young to stay out late,
I had seen sundaes more superb than this,
But not with the divine tranquillity
My mother's junkets had. It seemed to me
Their purity defied analysis.

Just once she made the junket pink, but I,
Craving vanilla, frowned at cochineal.
It went down fluently enough, but why
Fool with a classic product? Keep it real.
My eyes must have conveyed my faint disgust.
The visitant went back to being white
As if it had absorbed the years of light
It conquered spinning through the cosmic dust.

I grew up, ate the sundae any time
I felt like it, and never missed the bland
Sweet smoothness of the junket. Now I climb
Downstairs to see it coming in to land
There on the table as it used to do
So long ago, back when my life began.
I found it difficult to be a man.
This last feast seems more simple and more true.

Front Flip Half Twist

In the video from Wales, my granddaughter
Steps to the wall's edge. Just a yard below
The beach begins, a long way from the water.
A pause for thought. She then proceeds to throw
A cartwheel through the air, and, when she lands,
Stand upright on the sand, all done no hands.

She came to her miraculous mastery
Of this manoeuvre by a strict process –
She still insists it was no mystery –
Of more and more to reach down less and less
Until, one day, the finished thing was there,
Made manifest entirely in mid-air.

I who can fly no longer feel I'm flying
When I watch her describe that graceful arc,
So perfectly alive. I can't be dying
If I see this. The sky will not grow dark
While she spins through it, setting it alight,
Making my day by staving off the night.

Play it again. A poem that has taken
Its final form is radiant like this.
Beginnings left behind, but not forsaken,
Its history beyond analysis,
What starts by growing slowly, like a pearl,
Takes off and turns into a whirling girl.

Use of Space

My granddaughter has scored, for Modern Dance,
Good marks in all departments, with a nine
For "Use of Space". Give me another chance
And her certificate might well be mine.
I moved well at her age, and when I grew
I thought of Dance as something I could do.

I never could, of course. I merely flung
Myself about with untrained feet and hair.
No gift at all, except for being young,
And gradually that faded on the air
As I became another crumbling face
Scoring a pittance for his Use of Space.

Now I score zero. But because I've seen
Her switch to different corners of the room
Without, it seems, crossing the space between,
Delight reminds me time is a new broom:
It clears the floor our youngsters use to get
The compartmentalised certificate

That we'd have liked to have, but didn't put
The work into, and so did not deserve –
Although we might have been quite fleet of foot
And God knows that we would have had the nerve –
But we had other things to do and know.
Let her do this. Be glad, and let it go:

For you the Use of Space comes to an end
With your collapse into a spill of dust,
And you are for the wind and waves, my friend,
And all of this is timely, true and just.
The old ones disappear, the young dance on;
They use the space we make by being gone.

Photo File

The photographs in the manila folder
Are all of me when I was strong and bolder,
But now I'm old, and illness makes me older,
And winter's coming and the nights grow colder.

This photograph is me when I was swimming
At Inverell and sent the pebbles skimming
Across the river. Now my eyes are brimming
Because my arm aches and the light is dimming.

And in this one my wave of hair is showing
The gleam of Brylcreem, and my mother sewing
Has told me that I am a sheik, and going
To stun the girls when I have finished growing.

And here I am as the high-school debater.
A Cicero with an accelerator,
I talked too fast but I got better later.
That pimple left a noticeable crater.

The snaps of me when young are less narcotic,
I think, than those in which I look robotic,
Decked out by fame in various exotic
Bad hats and a fixed smirk that grew sclerotic.

I finished growing and the years went flying,
But there is no time now to waste time crying,
Although these pictures prove, beyond denying,
That once I was alive and not just dying.

Indeed because they show the treasure gleaming
Of good health I was granted beyond dreaming,
These constant posturings need no redeeming:
They are the substance. I am just the seeming.

The world I conquered is a tide retreating,
And with my maker there will be no meeting,
But look at this and see how time is fleeting:
Here, I am one year old. My heart is beating.

Time to pack up this packet and forget it.
The past would overwhelm me if I let it.
The clock ticks like a bomb. I didn't set it.
Let's just say there's a deadline and I met it.

Injury Time

This is a pretty trick the fates have played
On me, to make me think that I might die
Tomorrow, and then grant me extra time.
By now I feel that I have overstayed
My welcome. Every night I face the climb
Which might as well be straight into the sky:
The Himalayan slog upstairs to bed,
Placing my feet so carefully I seem
To tread on rolling logs, and there I dream
I come back down next morning, still not dead.
This nightly dream can turn out to be true
Only so long, and one day this notebook
Will lie untouched, to show how long it took
Silence to do what it was bound to do.

This Being Done

Behind the trees across the street the sun
Takes down its last pale disc. This being done,
No soft pale light is left for anyone.

There is a further comedown in the night.
Outside, unheard, asphalt is turning white:
White swarms of butterflies in the streetlight.

The morning comes, and through the spread of snow
In candy-coloured coats the children go.
Listen awhile and you can hear them grow.

Notes on the Text

Greatly gifted and prematurely cut down, James Elroy Flecker invented the Gardener in White at a time when death and decay, in order to fit the globalised imperial picture, were thought to need a touch of orientalist exoticism. Some of his rhythmic momentum, however, was permanently musical. Back in the days of black and white television, the BBC did an enchanting production of Flecker's *Hassan*, with Gielgud proving that there was nothing kitsch about the sonorities.

"Finch Conference": Phil Spector richly deserved his second-degree-murder rap but for anyone of my generation his tainted name still spells rhythmic power. The massed strings and guitars for "River Deep – Mountain High" gave so many of us the idea that the true object of popular music should be to move the male listener as close as possible to Tina Turner riding on the storm. Karsavina's little book *Theatre Street* is still always somewhere near me. Dynamism was part of her lyricism. At the time of writing, I am hooked by the way Zenaida Yanowsky can lean into a turn as if her speed was holding her upright. Every page of YouTube is a worm-hole to Andromeda.

Singing *Panis Angelicus* with his father in the gallery of Modena Cathedral, Pavarotti proved the truth of his unblushing contention that his gift came from God. He was a modest man, however: too modest to believe that the music he made gave him a right to be untrue to his obligations. Finally, as Cavaradossi in *Tosca*, he was so big that he had to sit down to be shot: but he still turned up for as long as his voice was true.

My poem about Beethoven is in seven parts to echo the structure of his greatest quartet. "They used to say he wrote only one opera, but he wrote the only opera." I first heard that idea from my dear friend Tony Locantro, who, back in the day when we first hit London, did so much to get me started on the love of serious music: and especially of the great operas. (As an apprentice A&R executive at EMI he had free access to the upcoming releases when they were still in "white label" form.) But for a long time much of the great chamber music was beyond me, and I am still finding out about it now, as the time approaches when it might not be so easy to read a book.

"Declaration of Intent": Back when I could still travel, in the dance halls of Buenos Aires I would study the way the tango masters, some of them a lot older than the hills, would maintain a hesitation step until the accumulated potential energy delivered them into a surge of forward movement. The *rallentando* hiatus gave the maestro's partner time to prepare for the searching reach of a long backward step. It often occurred to me that the parallel with writing poetry was very close. In a poem, to retard the impetus is often to prepare for power.

Carlos Fuentes has been gone now for several years but I still remember the humanist magnificence of the private library at his house in Mexico City. He said the place to see, in the historic Americas, was Oaxaca; but I never got there. The way he talked about Unamuno, however, I have remembered for all the time since. Even in old age, Carlos was a beautiful man in every respect, and the young women on my film team would sigh arias just from being in the same house.

I wrote the first drafts of "Not Forgetting George Russell" when I was locked up in the Closed Ward at Addenbrooke's after a psychotic reaction to steroids. The editor of the C-text of *Piers Plowman* was already dead by then but my conversations with him continued; as, indeed, they do today. I should add, however, that the poem didn't find its final form until I was back in the clear. The idea that scrambled brains are an aid to insight is not one I favour.

Finding the actual world quite bizarre enough, I never found surrealism interesting even when Magritte did it. But I can quite see how the subject of surrealism's validity might come up with some force if a surrealist as beautiful as Lee Miller gets herself photographed in Hitler's bathtub. Defending this poem from accusations of triviality, however, I would feel bound to say that she was almost certainly not concerned with making a surrealist statement but merely with having a bath, and that I was justified in calling her "sane". Later on she got clinically depressed about having taken her famous photographs in the concentration camps but that was a different part of the forest. There is room for an infinite amount of journalistic comment on these topics but perhaps it should start with the fact that Lee Miller was raped and given a dose of gonorrhoea at the age of seven.

Years ago now, on the daunting *favela* where my production team filmed a key sequence of *Postcard from Rio*, our local fixer made the mistake of wearing a conspicuous pair of white leather shoes. But the mistake was ours to give him his stipend in advance. He was murdered for it. The extreme tonal range of that city has haunted me ever since.

In "Aldeburgh Dawn", one of the last poems I began writing "on location", as it were, most of the factual points about the setting can be easily googled, but the mention of the Falaise Gap might be a mystery to younger readers, because it gives the name of a place to an event happily forgotten. The turkey shoot at Falaise, where the rockets fired by the Typhoons punched holes in the retreating German armour, was the true end for the *Wehrmacht* in the West. In Aldeburgh at night, and in the early morning, the continent seems not all that far away. The "Duck" was a DUKW, an amphibious vehicle.

Perhaps conserving his powers of effect, the imaginary narrator of "Tactics of the Air Battle" praises the superiority of the P-38 while neglecting to mention that it was limited by its short range *vis-à-vis* the Mustang (P-51). A better sky in which to look for the true glory of the twin-boom fighter was in the Pacific theatre, where Richard Bong won his forty victories. My device of the ghost pilot narrator enabled me to draw upon the enthusiasms of my childhood: a mental storehouse that fills, I am convinced, far in advance of any urge to write poetry, and goes dim only at the end of life.

Though I was never a true student of gymnastics, I vaulted well enough to be part of Sydney Technical High School's team that won the Pepsi Cola Shield. I mention this achievement here because the time for securing any further athletic triumphs is running out.

Letter to a Young Poet

First of all, give up if you can. Nobody who isn't neurotically driven should be in the game, because the chances of failure are too high, and the disappointments are too cruel. So we can safely assume that you are writing poetry because you must, and not just because you think it a more rewarding activity than stacking shelves. The latter assumption is statistically wrong anyway: the average stacked shelf is not only more useful to society than the average poem, it is actually superior as a work of art.

Thus committed by a burning, Miltonic compulsion to your lifetime's destiny, you will have already noticed that your work attracts more blame than praise, and more indifference than either. Train yourself to care less about the praise. You should work your new poem to perfection not because it will please more people that way – it might please fewer – but because in its finished state it will prove itself an independent artefact invulnerable even to your own doubts. If the poem has its own confidence, the day will come when you can look back on it and wonder how you did it. Usually that day, if it comes at all, comes soon; but it seldom comes immediately, so keep back anything you write until you are sure that it is really finished. Through this point runs the dividing line between the amateur and the professional. If the initial formative impulse is strong enough, there is a tendency to overlook soft spots and decide prematurely that the thing is done. Don't trust your enthusiasm until it dies down.

Geoffrey Grigson, a powerful editor in his day, thought that a poet should not keep a notebook. He claimed to be able to detect a "notebook poet" a mile off, in the way that the ageing Malcolm Muggeridge claimed that he could tell a woman who was on the pill by the dead light in her eyes.

Grigson was wrong, though his critical sympathies were so

acute that he was valuable even when he wasn't right. Keep a notebook: an ordinary quarto exercise book will do fine. If the observations you put into it are registered with sufficient precision, they might start to become poems, and can be transferred to your work book. The work book should be folio, so as to let you scan the whole poem as it builds. The work book can also be used for technical exercises. As a general rule nothing should go into your work book except poems asking to be finished, but few of them will get that far if you haven't mastered a range of manoeuvres for shifting the order of words about in service of a form. You can do without technical competence and still have a career, but you can't have very many finished poems, and no poems at all which will be shaped in unexpected directions by the set form you have chosen for them. Without technical expertise you can never surprise yourself, and thus will rarely surprise anybody else. There might be no need to master the villanelle or sestina, but you should certainly never stop practising your iambic pentameters and tetrameters, if only to have a name for something you have done accidentally. To get your caesura and anacrusis working smoothly, you can safely work on sonnets of pure nonsense as long as you resist the urge to give them titles and submit them to *Poetry* magazine.

In a properly kept work book there will always be a clear distinction between the technical mock-up and the real poem on its way towards completion. If the latter takes twenty years to get there, console yourself with the thought that your notebooks and work books are visible proof, if only to yourself, that waiting for inspiration is part of the process. When the final, provably inspired work is lifted from the work book and transferred to the computer, the process of eternal modification might very well seem to start all over again, but don't abandon it yet. Eventually the poem will tell you it is done by asking no more. Or else it will tell you it was misconceived by just lying there, saying nothing. Abandon it then.

Play a long game. To aid you in this judicious patience, it helps to have a brilliant, sensitive, and critically scrupulous friend to read your completed manuscript, but only if his objections are those that you would have made yourself, given time. If you find that what he really objects to is not mere detail but your basic individual tone, shoot him.

There is no reason to shoot critics as long as they quote you. Even the most hostile critic is working for you if he quotes you; and the chances are, he being his tin-eared self, that the line he picks out as self-evidently absurd or clumsy is one of your best, and will induce his readers to buy the very book on which he is ineptly pouring his brain-dead scorn. The dangerous critic is the bright, cultivated one who tells the world how wonderful you are. Begin learning straight away not to depend on his approval, which anyway he might be inclined not to repeat next time, lest he compromise his own renown for implacability. If you start thinking about your reputation, or even about your career as a poet, you are in the wrong frame of mind. What matters most is the poem, not the poet. A poet who worries because he hasn't been in any of the ritzier periodicals often enough lately would be better off busking his latest poem in the town square and seeing how it goes over. And there is always his personal website, as long as he remembers that everything written carefully for print should be written twice as carefully for the web. But if you need reminding to take pains, you shouldn't be doing this stuff anyway. A poem is something that never stops telling you to be careful until it's done: you get it started, go on developing it, and keep watching its tone until the whole thing sings.

To that end, if you feel the need of a role model, copy the sense of order that he brings to his phrases, and not the disorder with which he lived his life. If you are a male poet, there is nothing to be learned from how Robert Lowell, in his mania, stomped around pretending he was Hitler, or proposed to the air hostess on a trans-atlantic flight. Try to learn instead from how he put his images together in "The Quaker Graveyard in Nantucket". If you are a female poet, and lucky enough to be a lesbian, copy Elizabeth Bishop's verbal precision but don't imagine that her alcoholism helped her towards it. It didn't. As for Sylvia Plath, it wasn't her suicide that made her a great poet; just as Anne Sexton's suicide didn't make her Sylvia Plath. For poets of any gender, the idea that only an intense life can produce intense poetry is a very bad one. If saying interesting things doesn't strike you as an interesting enough activity, join the army.

In the periodicals and publishing houses, the best editors already know about most of the things I have advised you of; and the very best are usually poets themselves, so they have felt all this on the skin. That doesn't mean you should respect their opinion if they dislike your current poem, but with any editor it's always worth trying again with the next poem. There is plenty of bitchery among editors, and some of it is towards contributors: but all editors are united in their desire to print something by you if they find it good. The editor's position is a practical one: he or she is more concerned with printing something attractive to read than with helping to decide starting positions in the world-historical struggle towards immortality. You should have the same priorities. Nobody is asking you to descend to the level of show business, if that's the way you feel about the clueless punters; but if you can't bring yourself to write something readable, their fickle glance will move on.

If even a few people remember a line or two in a poem you wrote, you're not just getting there, you're there. That's it: and all the greater glory is mere vanity. When Raleigh bade farewell to the world's vanities – honoured rags, glorious bubbles – he put his best efforts into the poem with which he did it, and which no audience might ever read; a poem he crafted as if he were starting his life again, and had never fought the Spanish armada, or sailed to America, or dodged for his life when the Queen fell for him.

Seamus Heaney faithfully tending his creative writing classes at Harvard, and Philip Larkin stacking shelves in his library at Hull, were both trying to tell you something: even if the blaze of poetic glory descends on you, somewhere in the middle of it you should maintain the realisation that your status as a poet is a side issue. Nothing matters except your new poem. Is the thing that demanded to be written demanding to be read aloud? Does it make your mouth move when you read? You might feel childish if it does, but try to remember that this whole misbegotten adventure began when you were very young and said something clever. It made you famous in your family, which should be fame enough while you get on with the business of saying something clever again.

It's the task you were born to, or you think you were; and if it turns out that you were wrong, there are hundreds of other tasks that are poetic too, or can be made so if attended to with sufficient care and style. Your sense of dedication is one of the best things about you, so if you can't use it doing this, use it doing something else – just as long as you get enough spare time to go on reading poetry, the second best thing after writing it, as I'm sure you agree.

Cambridge, 2017